I0199687

# A Sourcebook of Nineteenth-Century American Sacred Music for Brass Instruments

*Joyful Noise*
frontispiece from a monotype
by Katherine Anderson

*Make a joyful noise unto the Lord, all the earth:*
*Make a loud noise, and rejoice, and sing praise. . .*
*With trumpets and sound of cornet*
*Make a joyful noise before the Lord, the King.*
– Psalm 98

***Soli Deo Gloria***

# A Sourcebook of Nineteenth-Century American Sacred Music for Brass Instruments

MARK J. ANDERSON

*Music Reference Collection, Number 59*

**GREENWOOD PRESS**
Westport, Connecticut • London

**Library of Congress Cataloging-in-Publication Data**

Anderson, Mark J., 1943–
A sourcebook of nineteenth-century American sacred music for brass instruments / Mark J. Anderson.
p. cm.—(Music reference collection, ISSN 0736–7740 ; no. 59)
Includes bibliographical references (p. ) and index.
ISBN 0–313–30380–0 (alk. paper)
1. Brass ensembles—19th century—History and criticism. 2. Brass instrument music—19th century—History and criticism. 3. Church music—United States—19th century. I. Title. II. Series.
ML933.A53 1997
788.9′171′00973—DC21 97–8763
MN

British Library Cataloguing in Publication Data is available.



Library of Congress Catalog Card Number: 97–8763
ISBN: 0–313–30380–0
ISSN: 0736–7740

First published in 1997

Greenwood Press, 88 Post Road West, Westport, CT 06881
An imprint of Greenwood Publishing Group, Inc.

10 9 8 7 6 5 4 3 2 1

The editor and publisher gratefully acknowledge the following for permission to use copyrighted materials:

Kenneth Kreitner, *Discoursing Sweet Music: Town Bands and Community Life in Turn-of-the-Century Pennsylvania*, University of Illinois Press. Copyright © 1990 by the Board of Trustees of the University of Illinois. Reprinted by permission of University of Illinois Press.

Richard D. Wetzel, *Frontier Musicians on the Connoquenessing, Wabash, and Ohio*, Ohio University Press. Copyright © 1976 by Richard D. Wetzel. Reprinted by permission of Richard D. Wetzel.

Every reasonable effort has been made to trace the owners of copyright materials in this book, but in some instances this has proven impossible. The author and publisher will be glad to receive information leading to more complete acknowledgments in subsequent printings of the book and in the meantime extend their apologies for any omissions.

# Contents

# Acknowledgements

Much of the material in this collection comes from manuscript collections. Grateful acknowledgement is made to the following for their permission to use materials from their collections: Old Economy Village Music Archives, Pennsylvania Historical and Museum Commission; the Manchester, New Hampshire Historic Association. Most of the published sources dating from the nineteenth-century were made available to me at the library of the Chatfield Band in Chatfield, Minnesota. The out-of-print and uncopyrighted collection of Bernard Pfohl was made available by Lillian Fort and Jonetta Conrad in North Carolina. The New York City Public Library provided material from their rare edition of Adelaide Fries': *Funeral Chorales of the Unitas Fratrum or Moravian Church*. The Moravian Congregation in Lititz, Pennsylvania provided the photograph of the trombone choir in the church belfry. Many of the pictures and information regarding the nineteenth-century musicians comes from publications of that century in the collection of the author. Anecdotal information and materials have been kindly provided by Tom and Dave Keehn, Paul Maybery, Ron Holz, Ralph Dudgeon and Claire Rowe. I am enormously grateful to my musician friends and colleagues for helping me by playing and singing the music in this collection: Barbara Pickhardt, Doris Blatter, and the choir of Christ's Lutheran Church; brass players: Don Burr, Carol Covas, Karl Kelbaugh, Ron Westervelt and Tom Keehn.

# Acknowledgments

# Introduction

Brass players are frequently called upon to play in church, especially for festival occasions. The repertoire is fairly predictable: Telemann, Purcell, Clarke, Greene, Stanley, Krebs, Bach, Handel; then Vaughan Williams, Hovhaness and a host of other twentieth-century writers. For many years I never thought much about the great, yawning chasm between the distant past and the present. Recent events have caused us to take a much closer look at the popular literature for brass in the nineteenth century. Some important things emerge from a past that has been made murky by our present biases. It is unfortunate that in mid-twentieth century many of us were taught an abhorrence for the perceived decadence of the "Victorian aesthetic of the Gilded Age." Perhaps more influential has been the increasingly strong current of secularism in the popular culture of the United States. In a negative reaction to the religious values of earlier generations we have foregone several important spiritual and aesthetic advantages. These include: an ability to understand sacred music at an intentional level and the loss of almost all of a fine and sometimes transcendent body of music: sacred music written and arranged for brasswinds in the United States from the mid-nineteenth century through the first decades of the twentieth century. A little of this music is well known among certain specialists but most of it has been completely lost and forgotten. What follows is a summary survey identifying the music and placing it within an historical context. It is hoped that this sourcebook will prove to be a useful collection of music to be used at appropriate times and places. Furthermore, it should also provide useful information about the music, the writers, and the players.

## MORAVIANS

There is an unbroken line of wonderful Moravian musicians, rooted in both the old *stadtpfeifer* and Lutheran hymn singing traditions, who began their musical life on these shores in the eighteenth century. In addition to survival, they were greatly dedicated to evangelism. Story has it that the sound of their horns deflected an Indian raid and that not long thereafter they were instructing the indigenous population in the fine art of chorale music for trombone choir. Imagine if you will a full voiced *posaunenchor* manned by converted Amerinds.

The zeal of the Moravians extended far beyond the Amerinds – they even reached out to Methodists. It seems that John and Charles Wesley were so impressed with the music of Moravians who were on the ship with them headed for America, that they continued their association with the Moravians and with German chorales when they returned to England.

On board the ship was a group of . . . Moravian missionaries. . . . These Moravian bretheren were enthusiastic hymn singers, and their hymnody made a deep impression upon the Wesleys. The English brothers remembered . . . when, during a severe storm that terrified most of the passengers, the Moravians calmly stood on the deck singing their hymns, entirely unperturbed by the raging storm and the towering waves. John Wesley began at once to study the hymnbooks of the Moravians, as attested by an entry in his journal . . . After his return to England [he] frequented the meetings of the Moravian bretheren . . . This association led to a crucial experience in Wesley's religious development, namely, his . . . 'conversion.' This occurred during a reading of Luther's Preface to the Epistle of the Romans, as described by Wesley in his journal:

**John Wesley**

'About a quarter before nine, while he was describing the change which God works in the heart through faith in Christ, I felt my heart strangely warmed. I felt I did trust in Christ, Christ alone for salvation; and an assurance was given me that He had taken away my sins, even mine and saved me from the law of sin and death.'

This might be called the basic text . . . for the whole movement of evangelical and revivalist hymnody. Note the emphasis on direct salvation through faith in Christ, the conviction of salvation coming as an emotional and heartwarming personal experience, and the feeling of elation resulting from the taking away of sin. This type of emotional reaction, this attitude toward conversion and salvation, and this basic imagery of sin and death, are the seeds out of which grew American folk hymnody, including the Negro spirituals.[1]

Moravian trombone choir

We shall witness the appropriation of Wesleyan musical taste later on in another important stream of fervent musical evangelism practiced by the Salvation Army. In the meantime, the Moravians continued to maintain their new world settlements and a rich musical life, even as they carried on their missionary work. The Northern Province of the Moravians was established in Pennsylvania in 1740. In Bethlehem, Pennsylvania, they organized an instrumental society known as the *Collegium Musicum* in 1744. The trombone choir of Central Moravian Church in Bethlehem remains a vital institution to this day.

The Southern Province of the Moravian Church is also of inestimable importance. By 1765 trombones were being used for festival occasions and for funerals in Salem (Winston-Salem), North Carolina. The players read from hand copied chorale books sent from Europe. In 1783 a cantata, *A Psalm of Joy,* was prepared for the first Independence Day celebration by J.F. Peter. In Salem the brass choir evolved into an ensemble of mixed winds during the course of the nineteenth century. By 1850 the trombone choir had given way to a family of valved brasswinds playing for civic as well as church functions. These Moravians then became the nucleus for some of the North Carolina regimental bands during the Civil War. During the war the bands of both the blue and the gray were called upon to provide music for church services conducted in the field as well as for the more commonly documented duties. We can be certain that the Moravians of both the North and the South contributed a great deal in their own bands and to other regimental bandsmen in demonstrating the usefulness of a brass ensemble in the playing of sacred music. "The bugle has sounded church call and the band have commenced playing. . . . It would seem strange to you to have a full brass band to play for a service. But I assure you it is excellent and it is very appropriate."[2]

**Daniel Crouse in 1862**

**Bernard Pfohl in 1950**

After the war the surviving bandsmen returned home carrying the burden of their service. In Salem, Daniel Crouse who had played baritone horn in the 26th North Carolina regimental band, started up the Salem Cornet Band. Many of their arrangements of hymns were prepared by Edward Leinbach, brother of Julius, another veteran of the 26th North Carolina Band. These arrangements were used in hand-copied manuscript editions for many years until printed books were prepared from them in 1927. The printed materials were edited by Bernard Pfohl, a remarkable man whose service in the Salem band began in 1879 and continued until the 1950's. He was tutored by both Daniel Crouse

CHORALES AND TUNES

Used by the Bands of

The Moravian Church

**The cover page of Pfohl's collection**

and Edward Leinbach. Mr. Pfohl wrote a book entitled: *The Salem Band* (privately published, Winston-Salem, N.C., 1953), from which most of this history of the Moravian tradition is taken.[3]

The music Bernard Pfohl so carefully prepared and published in 1927 is a collection entitled: *Chorales and Tunes Used by the Bands of the Moravian Church*. It consists of 82 arrangements of Moravian chorales, Christmas hymns, and patriotic tunes. It is a magnificent collection and has been the inspiration for several later collections. Not included in the collection are the Leinbach arrangements made of popular hymns outside the Moravian tradition, although Bernard Pfohl has written that such arrangements existed.

Popular hymnody in the United States flowered under the influence of Lowell Mason (1792-1872) of Boston, Thomas Hastings (1784-1872) in New York City, and William Bradbury (1816-1868) of Maine who, along with Mason, Hastings and George Root, taught in the Normal Institutes - "a scientifically improved version of the old singing schools."[4] Other popular although more regional collections included William Walker's *Southern Harmony* and Benjamin White's *Sacred Harp*. These collections both filled a need and created a desire for more popular hymns. After the Civil War the work was taken up by a younger group of writers.

**Lowell Mason about 1830**

According to Pfohl: "The band played *Hold the Fort For I Am Coming, Rescue the Perishing, Precious Name*, etc., songs arranged by E.W. Leinbach."[5] All three of these popular gospel hymns are to be found in a collection compiled by Ira Sankey, entitled: *Gospel Hymns Combined* (John

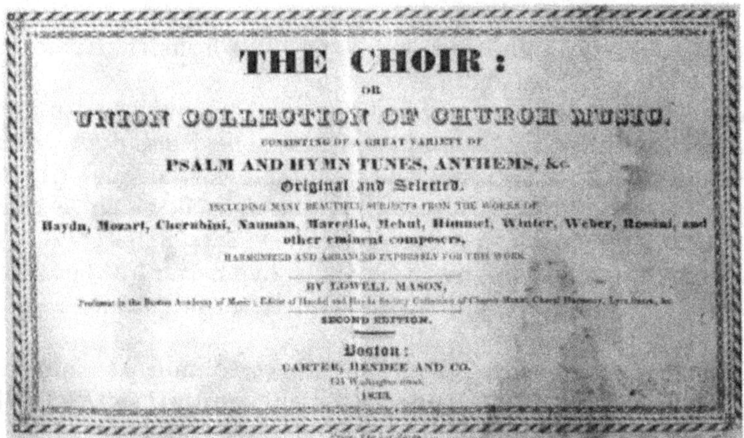

THE CHOIR:
OR
UNION COLLECTION OF CHURCH MUSIC,
CONSISTING OF A GREAT VARIETY OF
PSALM AND HYMN TUNES, ANTHEMS, &c.
Original and Selected.
INCLUDING MANY BEAUTIFUL SUBJECTS FROM THE WORKS OF
Haydn, Mozart, Cherubini, Nauman, Marcello, Mehul, Himmel, Winter, Weber, Rossini, and other eminent composers,
HARMONIZED AND ARRANGED EXPRESSLY FOR THIS WORK.
BY LOWELL MASON,
SECOND EDITION.
Boston:
CARTER, HENDEE AND CO.
1833.

One of Mason's books, published in 1833.

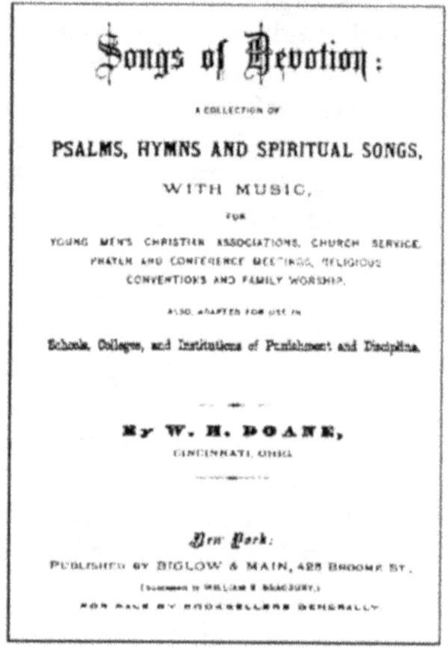

Songs of Devotion:
A COLLECTION OF
PSALMS, HYMNS AND SPIRITUAL SONGS,
WITH MUSIC,
FOR
YOUNG MEN'S CHRISTIAN ASSOCIATIONS, CHURCH SERVICE, PRAYER AND CONFERENCE MEETINGS, RELIGIOUS CONVENTIONS AND FAMILY WORSHIP.
ALSO, ADAPTED FOR USE IN
Schools, Colleges, and Institutions of Punishment and Discipline.
By W. H. DOANE,
CINCINNATI, OHIO.
New York:
PUBLISHED BY BIGLOW & MAIN, 425 BROOME ST.
(SUCCESSORS TO WILLIAM B. BRADBURY.)
FOR SALE BY BOOKSELLERS GENERALLY.

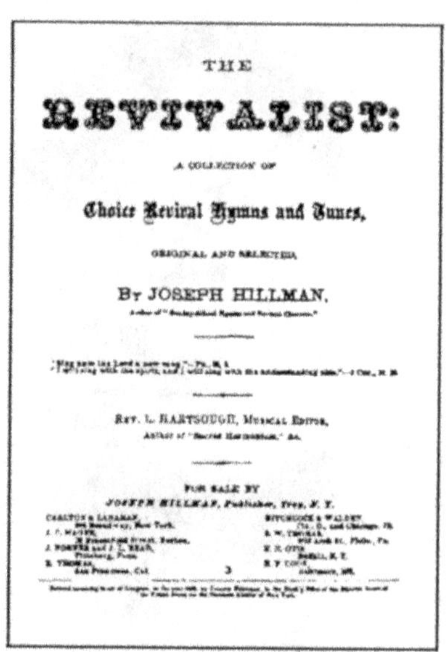

THE
REVIVALIST:
A COLLECTION OF
Choice Revival Hymns and Tunes,
ORIGINAL AND SELECTED.
BY JOSEPH HILLMAN,
REV. L. HARTSOUGH, MUSICAL EDITOR,
FOR SALE BY
JOSEPH HILLMAN, Publisher, Troy, N. Y.

Two popular nineteenth-century hymn books, 1870 and 1869.

Church & Co., Cincinnati, 1879). *Hold the Fort* was written by Philip Bliss and first published in one of his own collections of gospel hymns. The metaphor is based on an incident that occurred during the Civil War. "*Res-*

*cue the Perishing* . . . is sung not only in . . . church prayer meetings . . . but in Salvation Army camps, in . . . Sons of Temperance Meetings, and in the rallies of every . . . organization that seeks the lost . . . "[6] The tune was written by W.H. Doane in 1870 who also wrote the music for *Precious Name*.[7]

It is clear that Edward Leinbach and the Moravians were fond of the same popular hymnody as were Americans of other denominations. No wonder! The music was derivative of the musical traditions which had been central to Moravian life for centuries. It is ironic to note that most of the Moravians of the nineteenth century were probably unaware of the direct connection between this popular hymnody and their own musical history.

In reviewing the hymnbooks from those years, the names most frequently encountered are Ira Sankey, Philip Bliss, James McGranahan and George Stebbins."The . . . Sankey hymns were used in Sunday schools and revival services. Mr. E. W. Leinbach . . . arranged quite a collection of these hymns for the . . . band to play . . . the new band members made more copies and put them into book form."[8]

## EVANGELISTS

Ira Sankey

The names Moody and Sankey still ring with familiarity in the heartland consciousness of the United States. This team of evangelists continued the tradition of camp and revival meetings that had begun during the "Great Awakening" of the late eighteenth century on into the post Civil War era. Dwight Moody (1837 - 1899) was the preacher and organizer while Ira Sankey (1840 - 1908) was the singer, accompanist and hymn writer.

Religious revival meetings were a . . . favorite . . . and no revival team compared in popularity to Dwight L. Moody and Ira D. Sankey. Moody in 1875 was the 'rising young tycoon of the revival trade as Andrew Carnegie was of the steel trade or John D. Rockefeller of oil.' He was the revivalist who coupled business-like methods with 'the old fashioned gospel,' and his success was enormous. In this he was substantially aided by Ira D. Sankey, who took charge of the music and contributed stirring solo renditions of popular gospel hymns.[9]

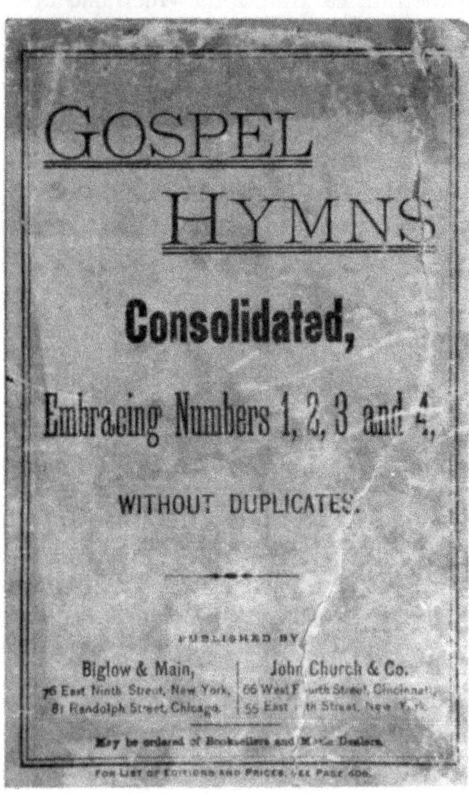


*Gospel Hymns* cover, 1883

Their publications of popular hymns for "gospel meetings and other religious services" began in the 1870s with *Gospel Hymns and Sacred Songs* and continued through six volumes until 1892. The collections were entitled: *Gospel Hymns No. 2; Gospel Hymns No. 3*, etc. Eventually they began publishing them in combined volumes entitled: *Gospel Hymns Combined; Gospel Hymns Consolidated*, etc. The books were enormously popular, being sold at revival and camp meetings all over the world as well as during the evangelistic missions of Moody and Sankey themselves. Lowell Mason's earlier hymn book, *Carmina Sacra*, of 1841 is said to have sold more than 400,000 copies.[10] Sankey's collection entitled *Sacred Songs and Solos* sold fifty million copies![11] The authors, compilers and editors of these collections included Philip Bliss, James McGranahan and George Stebbins as well as Ira Sankey. Although it may seem incredible to those of us living a century later, these popular hymns were the source of a high percentage of the "top forty" of those days.

They carried the more emotional and less cultivated element of religious people off its feet, and furnished for a time the familiar songs of vast numbers hitherto unacquaintedwith hymns . . . The new melodies . . . were whistled by the man on the street. . . . Easy, catchy, sentimental, swaying with a soft or a martial rhythm and culminating in a taking refrain; calling for no musical knowledge to understand and no skill to render them; inevitably popular, with the unfailing appeal of clear melody.[12]

In 1887 the John Church Company, publishers of the Sankey *Gospel Hymns*, brought out the collection: *Gospel Hymns Consolidated, arranged for the Cornet* by S.C. Hayslip. These were "For use in Sabbath Schools, Gospel Meetings, and all Revival Services." In a publisher's note the justification for the collection is made:

It is believed that the usefulness of Gospel Hymns Consolidated, will be very much increased by this arrangement of its melodies for Cornet. The Cornet is a powerful leader, and in large assemblies it is especially effective in keeping the Congregation up to time and pitch. In arranging this work for the Cornet, those Keys have been selected which admit of the greatest ease and facility of execution. A Piano or Organ played from the regular Edition will agree perfectly with the Cornet played from this one.[13]

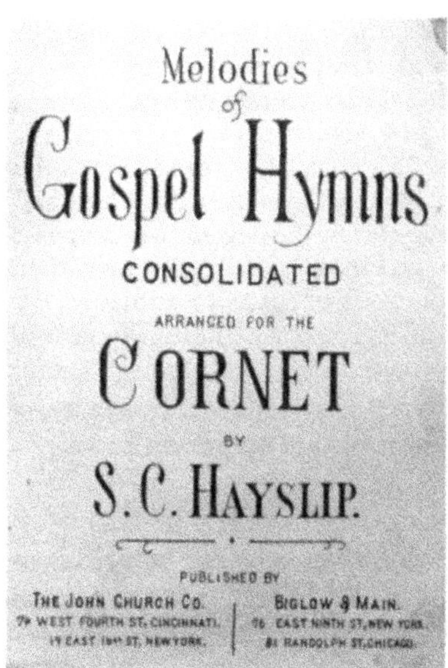


**Title page from the 1887 cornet edition arranged by Hayslip**

The collection includes tunes for 426 hymns. Cornet in A is used as well as cornet in Bb in an attempt to keep the instrument in key signatures having the least intonation problems for the standard nineteenth century instruments.

Bandleader George Ives and his son Charles were acutely aware of intonation "problems" for brass instruments and also in congregational singing:

Exception has been taken. . .to my using . . . suggestions of old hymns. . . . As one . . . professor told me, 'Imagine, in a symphony . . . hearing suggestions of . . . a Moody and Sankey hymn!' . . . His opinion is based on something he'd . . . never heard . . . or experienced. . . . – and I had the chance of hearing them big. . . I remember, when I was a boy – at the outdoor Camp Meeting services . . . all the farmers, their families and field hands, for miles around, would come afoot

**George Ives with his cornet, c. 1864**

**Charles Ives in 1892**

or in their farm wagons. I remember how the great waves of sound used to come through the trees – when things like *Beulah Land, Woodworth, Nearer My God To Thee, The Shining Shore, Nettleton, In the Sweet Bye and Bye* and the like were sung by thousands of 'let out' souls. The music notes and words on paper were about as much like what they 'were' (at those moments) as the monogram on a man's necktie may be like his face. Father, who led the singing, sometimes with his cornet or his voice, . . . sometimes in the quieter hymns with a French horn or violin, would always encourage people to sing their own way. Most of them knew the words and music (theirs) by heart and sang it that way. If they threw the poet or the composer around a bit, so much the better for the poetry and the music. . . . the way, at an outdoor meeting . . . with no instrumental accompaniment except a cornet . . . the fervor of the feeling would at times, especially on reaching the Chorus of many of those hymns, throw the key higher, sometimes a whole tone up – though Father used to say it [was] more often about a quarter tone up – and . . . Father had a sliding cornet made so that he could rise with them and not keep them down.[14]

The hymns from the Sankey collections used by George Ives had been arranged for brass ensemble not only by Moravian Edward Leinbach of the Salem Band, but by others as well. T.H. Rollinson, cornet player, bandleader, church organist, composer and arranger in Waltham, Massachusetts arranged some of the Moody and Sankey hymns into a *Grand Religious Fantasia* for band published by the J.W. Pepper Company in 1901.

The J.W. Pepper Company also published a collection of 70 sacred pieces for band or smaller brass ensemble based on the popular Moody and Sankey

70 SACRED PIECES. FOR FULL BAND.

Suitable for Religious Celebrations, Camp Meetings, Sunday School Excursions, Revival Meetings, Etc.

# Gospel Hymns Sacred Band Book

## Playable as Quartette, Sextette, Quintette or Octette,

WITH AD LIB. PARTS FOR 20.

This Band Book contains a brilliant selection of Popular Hymns and Sunday School Pieces taken from Moody and Sankey's Popular Gospel Hymns—a work known and used in every part of this hemisphere. Our reasons for making the selection entirely from this work are simple, its contents are familiar to every churchgoer and scholar, and a band engaged for a church celebration of any character can use this book with absolute confidence in the reception of its work. An important feature of the arrangement of each piece contained in this book, consists in the fact that it is printed in a key to correspond with the vocal arrangement, so that while a band is doing duty as a great church organ, the audience can join in and sing, producing the most effective combination that one could imagine. The harmony is identical with that used in the vocal collection, and when using this splendid work, there is nothing to prevent a full Brass Band taking part in every character of church gatherings.

**FOR QUARTETTE OR SEXTETTE,** select your combination from the following instruments playing:

**SOPRANO OR MELODY PARTS**—Solo or Eb Clarinet, Solo or 1st Bb Clarinet, Solo or 1st Bb Cornet, Solo Bb Cornet, Solo Alto.

**ALTO PARTS**—2d Bb Clarinet, 1st Bb Cornet, 1st Alto, 2d Tenor.

**TENOR PARTS**—2d Cornet, 2d Alto, 1st Tenor, Baritone.

**BASS PARTS**—Tenor (from Bb Bass part), Baritone (from Bb Bass part), Bb Bass, Eb Bass.

For extra parts up to full arrangement any leader can add instruments that play the different voice parts, or as he may be able to obtain players. In all cases piccolo and drum parts are to be added at pleasure.

As a **Quintette** (5), use any extra solo or melody part as a relief. As a **Sextette** (6), use any extra instruments playing Air or Soprano, and one to assist Tenor voice part. As a **Septette** (7), use extra instruments for Soprano, Alto and Tenor voice parts. As **Octette** (8), use extra instruments for Soprano, Alto, Tenor and Bass, or double each part, making a double quartette.

**FULL INSTRUMENTATION, 20 Books,** viz.: Piccolo, Solo Eb Clarinet, 1st (or Solo) and 2d Bb Clarinets, 1st and 2d Eb Cornets, Solo, 1st and 2d Bb Cornets, Solo, 1st and 2d Eb Altos, 1st and 2d Bb Tenors, Bb Baritone, Bb Bass, 1st and 2d Eb Basses, Snare and Bass Drums. The Solo Bb Cornet, Solo Eb Clarinet, Solo Bb Clarinet and Solo Alto contain all the melody, and are arranged similar to the Bb Cornet, so that **this book can be led by any of the above Solo parts.** We publish the 1st and 2d Tenors, Baritone, Bb Bass in both Bass and Treble Clefs. State, when you order, which Clef you desire.

CONTENTS

Arlington.
Autumn.
Belmont.
Beulah Land.
Blessed Home Land.
Boylston.
Brightly Gleams Our Banner.
Child of Sin and Sorrow.
Come, Ye Disconsolate.
Coronation.
Cross and Crown.
Dennis.
Depth of Mercy.
Dundee.
Eternity Is Drawing Nigh.
Evan.
Expostulation.
Go Work in My Vineyard.
Guide Me O Thou Great [Jehovah.
Hamburg.
Hebron.
Home of the Soul.
Home Over There.
I Am Coming to the Cross.
I Am Sweeping Thro' the Gates
I Left It All with Jesus.
I Love to Tell the Story.
I'm a Pilgrim.
In the Presence of the King.
Italian Hymn.
Jesus Is Mighty to Save.
Jesus, Lover of My Soul.
Jesus Shall Reign.
Lead Me On.
Lord Will Provide.
My Ain Countree.
New Haven.
Not Half Has Ever Been Told.
Nothing But Leaves.
Oh, How He Loves.
Oh, What Are You Going to Do?
Old Hundred.
One Sweetly Solemn Thought.
On Jordan's Stormy Banks.
Only for Thee.
Onward Christian Soldiers.
Pleyel's Hymn.
Rockingham.
Rock of Ages.
Safe in the Arms of Jesus.
Say! Are You Ready.
Seymour.
Shall We Meet?
Shirland.
Sinner Forgiven.
Song of Salvation.
Sun of My Soul.
Sweet Hour of Prayer.
There Is a Fountain.
Till He Come.
To-Day.
Triumph By and By.
Valley of Blessing.
We Shall Sleep, But Not Forever.
What a Friend We Have Jesus.
Where Is Thy Refuge?
Whiter Than Snow.
Wilmont.
Wondrous Love.
Yield Not to Temptation.

Playable with Solo and 1st Bb Cornets, 1st and 2d Altos, Tenor, Baritone and Tuba, up to full band.

SAMPLE Bb OR Eb CORNET PARTS MAILED FREE FOR 8c. IN STAMPS

**Single book, 50c. 16 books at one time, $5.00.**

**Any order for more than 16 books, 30c. each additional book.**

J.W. Pepper advertisement including many of the same titles published in the cornet edition of *Gospel Songs*.

hymns. This collection came out in 1887, the same year the John Church Company published the cornet leader's book. There is no record of the number of these books sold, but since the publication was issued in 1887 and the book still warranted almost a half-page advertisement in the annual catalog of 1907 we can guess that sales were brisk.[15]

## THE SAINTS

*Jesus, Lover of my Soul,* a song out of the *Sankey Hymnal,* is changed by the Shouting Baptists of Trinidad into an unmistakably African song. And . . . in a great many parts of the West Indies, all the Protestant pseudo-Christian religious songs are called 'sankeys.' [16]

The spread of religious instruction among the Negroes coincided with the rise of the camp-meeting movement. As we know from . . . contemporary sources, Negroes as well as whites took part in the early camp meetings. . . . there is no doubt that the same songs were sung by both races. . . . The Southern evangelist Lucius Bellinger wrote of one of his camp meetings: 'The negroes are out in great crowds, and sing with voices that make the woods ring.' [17]

In his fine book, *Brass Bands and New Orleans Jazz* (Louisiana State University Press, 1977), William Schafer notes that country bands were one of the sources feeding the New Orleans black brass-band tradition, and that they served as an outlet for black musicians following the Civil War. Schafer quotes extensively from the research done by Frederick Ramsey, Jr. in producing recordings for Folkways (FP650):

The essential point to be noted, in connection with all the Negro brass bands formed shortly after Emancipation, is that they played without instruction, and picked up their tunes by ear: 'Well, I tell you how it was. It was just . . . you take a fellow, he'll set down, if he hearin' 'bout a sing, a hymn . . . or hear anything like that. Well, after he got it prompt in his mind, then he'll pick up his horn. Then he'll try to play it, you see? That's the way it was. They first start playing spirituals . . . got them at the church. They go way back . . . '

The music played by members of these early plantation brass bands was based on song - they blew *singing horns.* Their repertoire came, not from the white man's stock of . . . sheet music, but from church and secular songs. From the church side, they played spirituals, jubilees, and possibly, some early chants. They had probably sung them in their churches and homes before blowing them through their horns.

. . . The practices of these rough plantation bands indicate one musical influence that was as strong in New Orleans as in the country – the powerful and exuberant vocal music of the black churches. Just as country musicians 'caught' by ear spirituals and hymns, brass bands in New Orleans would play 'head' arrangements of simple hymn tunes like 'What a Friend We Have in Jesus' or 'In the Upper Garden,' or they would read rudimentary arrangements sketched from four-part vocal music in church hymnals.[18]

The music played by the black street bands in New Orleans from about 1870 to 1890 has been called archaic jazz by Gilbert Chase. He describes the scene with a band marching in a funeral procession to the cemetery playing slow dirges and adaptations of old hymns. On the return, the music would get "hot" in a tune like *Oh, Didn't He Ramble,*[19] or *When the Saints Go Marchin' In.*[20]

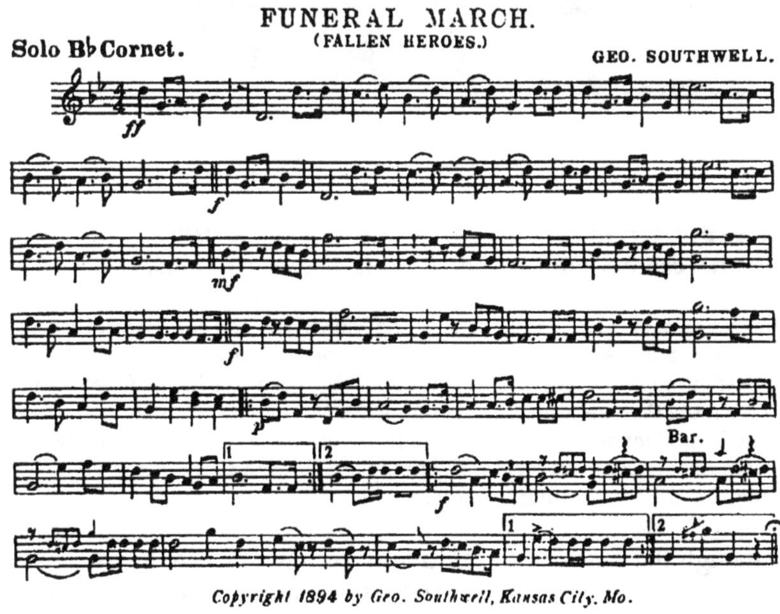


**Published version of a New Orleans funeral march**

## HARMONISTS

A group of dissenting German Protestants that immigrated to the United States during the nineteenth century was the communal Harmony Society

**Members of the Economy Band c. 1897**

founded by George Rapp. They arrived in 1804 and remained a viable group for about a century until the Society was dissolved in 1906.

> The extent of contact made between the Moravians and the Harmonists is not fully known, but there is little doubt that some of the Harmonists knew about and greatly admired the Moravians. . . . Frederick Rapp [adopted son of George Rapp] 'read for more than an hour an account of the Moravians' . . . in lieu of a Sunday sermon. The 'General Economy,' the name given to the communitarian system of the Moravians, may even have influenced the selection of the name given to the Harmonists' third community - Economy.[21]

Although the music of the Harmony Society nowhere approaches the quality and quantity of the Moravians, the archives maintained at Old Economy Village are an important source of extant exempla of additional sacred music for brass during this era. Perhaps as a result of their "closed door" policies versus the evangelistic fervor of some of the other traditions, the largest part of their instrumental collection was devoted to secular music. The most interesting sacred brass music surviving in the Old Economy archive is that from the period when Jacob Rohr was the bandmaster – from the 1870s to the early 90s. Although he was a German immigrant, Rohr was hired by the Harmonists and was not a member of the commune. "There are few records which show that Rohr purchased

**Manuscript of solo cornet part for *Pleyel's Hymn* courtesy of the Pennsylvania Historical and Museum Commission**

music for the ... Band. He appears to have arranged most of the repertoire himself." [22] Most of the extant sacred music manuscripts are for cornets, altos, baritones and bass although by 1889 they had added piccolo, Eb and Bb clarinets.

The catalog of music in the Economy archive includes brass ensemble arrangements of: *Lobe den Herren; Jesus Meiner Zuversicht; Jauchzet ihr Christ;* and a perennial favorite of brass bands during the era, *Pleyel's Hymn* (here with variations for cornet), all in manuscript. Published music in the collection includes: Rossini's *Stabat Mater* in an arrangement published as a special edition of C. Boose's Military Journal of 1869; *Joy to the World* (Grand Sacred Potpourri) from Barnhouse in 1894; *Providence* from Fischer in 1899; as well as at least half-dozen additional sacred works for mixed winds.

John Duss assumed control of the Economy Band in the 1890s and most of the arrangements from then on were for the typical wind band as published by Fischer, Barnhouse, and other commercial publishers, as well as a sprinkling of works and arrangements including a *Gloria* by the rather eccentric Duss.

## DIGNAM

In 1862 when Connecticut Yankee George Ives began his Civil War service as a 17-year-old bandleader, a 35 year old British immigrant named Walter Dignam also took up the baton, but for a New Hampshire Regiment. Dignam had settled in Manchester, New Hampshire in the 1840s and returned there after the war. In addition to being a band leader, Eb cornet virtuoso, composer and arranger, he also had a 28-year career as organist and choir director of the Roman Catholic Church in Manchester.

The fine collection[23] of 1850s manuscript band books in the Manchester Historical Association includes Dignam's arrangements of: *Rest Spirit, Rest; May Heaven's Grace; Old Hundred; St. Martins;* and *Hamburg*. It is fascinating to note that the collection also includes the *Marcia De Sacra* from Meyerbeer's *Le Prophete*. John Dwight, never a particular friend of brass bands, reported favorably on the performance of this march by a band of 1,000 under the direction of Patrick Gilmore at his *Peace Jubilee* of 1869.[24,25] Miscellaneous works in the collection include a Mass (*Messe On Second Ton)* scored for Violins 1 & 2, C clarinet, 1 & 2 Cornets and Bass. The clarinet doubles the first violin while the cornets double the lower voices with the second violin.

***St. Martins:*** **A section of the page from the cornet manuscript book of Walter Dignam. Courtesy Manchester Historic Association**

## THE EQUINUNK BAND OF REVEREND ALBERTI

In his recent book *Discoursing Sweet Music* [26] Kenneth Kreitner cites the Equinunk, Pennsylvania band as being unique because of its close association with a church. Within the area of his study he found that, "... bands were traditionally regarded as purely secular organizations, improper for religious purposes."[27] However the nineteenth-century town bands existed as secular organizations within a society having much greater involvement with established churches than is true at the close of the twentieth-

**The Equinunk Band c. 1898 from the collection of Hazel Peake. Courtesy University of Illinois Press**

century. Furthermore there existed many ethnic bands which were organized within churches.

Charles W. Alberti was the minister at the Methodist Episcopal Church in Equinunk from 1896 to 1901. As in many small hamlets and villages, the church was central to life in the community and the citizens rarely worried themselves much about fine distinctions between profane and sacred. Reverend Alberti was in his thirties when he organized the Equinunk Cornet Band in late 1896. Kreitner quotes passages from the Honesdale *Citizen* wherein the Equinunk correspondent asks only for deliverance from the sounds of the fledgling band. By the end of December, another report, this time on the band's debut on Christmas night, is favorable.[28] Such progress in a short time, considering the fact that Reverend Alberti was also in the midst of the Advent season and preparing for Christmas is certainly a testimony to his ability as a musician, band leader and teacher, as well as in indication of the dedication of his young bandsmen. Although no program survives, it is probably safe to make the assumption that since their gestation period coincided with Advent and they had a Christmas night debut, the band probably learned to play some Christmas hymns and carols.

## MORE EVANGELISM

Moody and Sankey took their revival on a successful tour to Great Britain in 1873 – just about the time a man named Fries started using his own little brass band to evangelize in an unauthorized manner for the Salvation Army of General William Booth. General Booth had been a Methodist and well acquainted with the Protestant hymnody handed down in the Lutheran–Moravian–Methodist traditions. It didn't take him long to authorize the unauthorized. By the 1880s brass bands (especially in the British model of *all* brass) become and still remain indelibly connected with the Salvationists on both sides of the Atlantic.

As with the Moravians, the principal concern of the Salvation Army is evangelism. The intensity of this focus along with a sense of insulation from secular society has tended sometimes to work at cross purposes with the goals of both groups. It has been a serious loss to the world that the best music of these men and women has been so little known for such a long time. The reputation of the Moravians has been growing since about mid–twentieth century, but mainly in conjunction with their relationship to the European *art* music of the eighteenth and nineteenth centuries. The Salvationists have been less well appreciated. This may have been caused by the early tension between the Salvation Army and other Christian churches which continued into the early twentieth century.

Prior to 1900, virtually all of the Salvation Army Band music was written and published in England. There was a brief appearance of an *American Band Journal* in 1898, but there was no regular input from our side of the Atlantic until 1928. In his fine tribute to the New York Staff Band on their 100th anniversary in 1987, Ronald Holz points out that during this period the repertoire of the band was augmented by "unauthorized" works.[29] Nonetheless, the music played by most of the bands from the 1880s to the 1920s consisted mainly of arrangements that would have sounded familiar to anyone in this country who wasn't deaf: hymns and marches for

**This page from an early Salvation Army Band Journal was found in the case of a nineteenth-century cornet originally owned by a bandsman in New Paltz, New York.**

brass band. Indeed, the Salvation Army bandsmen in Danbury, Connecticut, were trained by a Civil War veteran of the Union Army, George Ives, prior to his death in 1894. Later Charles Ives bequeathed us a setting of Vachel Lindsay's *General Booth Enters Into Heaven*.[30]

From the subject period right to the present day Salvation Army composers and arrangers have been developing a tradition of sacred music that many of us never even knew existed. The work is beautiful and worth seeking out through the many excellent recordings of the Army. The Salvation Army has also served as a training ground for numerous outstanding brass players and teachers. If you ask around, you'll find many who will say: "Sure – so and so was brought up in the Salvation Army and you know what a great player *(s)he* is!"

One of the reasons for the obscurity of this fine music was the control maintained in distribution. Little of the music was available to anyone other than the Salvation Army until fairly recently. Now good music of the Salvation Army is available to the rest of us, which is only proper – after all it all comes from the same place.[31] It should be stressed that the brass music of the Salvation Army is a dynamic tradition constantly evolving since its beginnings during the last century.

## INSTRUMENTS

During the second half of the nineteenth century the instrumentation of the brass ensembles was not the same as today. The number and kind of instruments was quite different than either our modern brass quintet or brass choir. Among modern brass ensembles, those most closely resembling the nineteenth-century groups are the present brass bands which follow the traditions of the Salvation Army and the "British" brass bands.

### Sopranos

The soprano voice was not a modern trumpet, but a cornet. The cornets of that time produced a sound that is quite different from the modern trumpet and most modern cornets. In general, the tubing of the older cornets was usually tapered or "conical bored" through most of its length while a trumpet has a much greater percentage of straight or slightly tapered tubing. The mouthpieces tended to have sharper rims and more funnel-shaped rather than bowl-shaped cups. Because of these differences, the older cornets had a much softer and more "mellow" tone - nowhere near the "brilliant" sound of a modern trumpet. These instruments were usually present in two pitches: Eb and Bb. The Eb cornet was the true soprano of the group, although solo work was almost always shared between the Eb and Bb cornets. Usually there was one Eb cornet and two Bb cornets in smaller bands (6-8 players), increasing to two and and two in medium-sized bands (9-14 players). The C.G. Conn company featured a Bb cornet with a "C" attachment, especially for use in in church.

# THE WONDER SOLO CORNET!

**With Vocal "C" Attachment.**

The cornet player who desires to use his instrument in the church choir or with the Piano or Organ and not be compelled to transpose the music, but play it just as it is written, will find this Vocal "C" attachment an invaluable adjunct to this instrument. The cornet in Bb and A is positively the same as the Wonder Solo Cornet except the valve slides which are made shorter so that the cornet will be in tune with itself when the "C" attachment is used. When the Cornet is used in Bb and A the Vocal attachment is removed and the tuning slide inserted in its place.

Instructions for the use of the Wonder Solo Cornet with the Vocal attachment:

To use the Cornet in "C" remove the tuning slide and insert in its place the "C" attachment, shove up the valve slides and use the Bb shank in the attachment. To use the cornet in Bb and A, replace the tuning slide and draw the valve slides to the mark indicated.

Each instrument is furnished with two mouthpieces, music-holder, piston wiper and water key. Cornets are complete in handsome velvet and satin-trimmed cases, and are furnished with the Hoch patent bell mute, and are sent for six days' trial and approval.

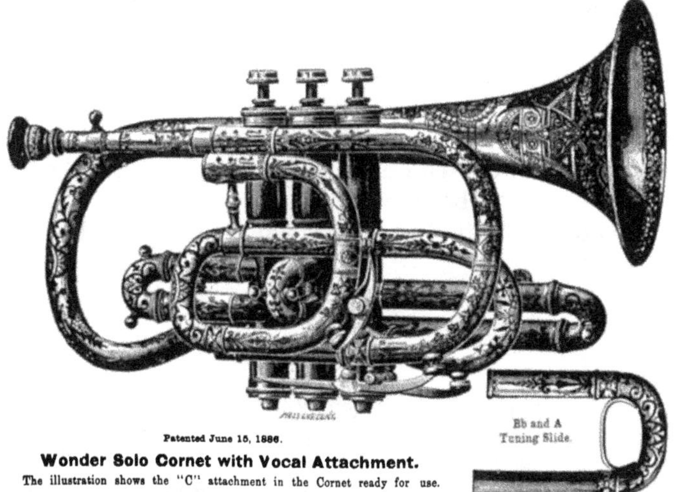


Patented June 15, 1886.

**Wonder Solo Cornet with Vocal Attachment.**

The illustration shows the "C" attachment in the Cornet ready for use.

**Finish of the Wonder Solo Cornet with Vocal Attachment. Prices given on Application.**

Triple silver-plated, elaborately engraved, burnished finish, inside of bell gilded, engraving spot gilded, gold points, complete in Morocco covered, Satin and Velvet lined case, with mute and water reservoir.

Triple silver-plated, elegantly engraved, burnished finish, inside of bell gilded, engraving spot gilded, gold points—complete in an elegant case.

Triple silver-plated, engraved, burnished finish and gilded bell, complete in an elegant case.

Brass, highly finished, engraved, complete in case.

In perfecting the above cornet for Solo and Orchestra use, or with the Voice, it has been our special effort to provide an easy blowing, superior tone, and even register. The instruments made by Mr. Conn can be forced to double *fortissimo* without changing the quality of the tone, and without the disagreeable Trumpet *blare* so destructive to artistic efforts, and always found in cornets not a CLEAR BORE. The upper register of the cornet can be reached with remarkable ease, and the tones sustained to the faintest *diminuendo* with scarcely an effort. His cornets are used by the principal Soloists, and are guaranteed to be the *best corne made in the world.*

**C. G. CONN, - - - - ELKHART, INDIANA,**

**AND WORCESTER, I ASS.**

**C.G. Conn advertisement for "church" cornet c. 1887**

**Altos**

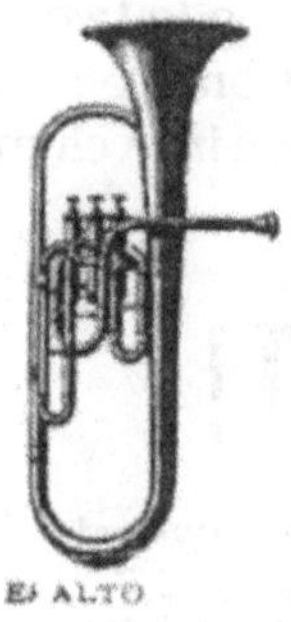

Alto lines were played by two or three alto horn players. These instruments were part of the Saxhorn family invented by the Belgian Adolph Saxe in the 1840s. The altos were either designed and built as upright horns (bell up rather than to the front) or in over-the-shoulder models for marching. The horns were pitched in Eb and were conically bored, producing a very mellow sound. Unlike the French horn (the modern alto voice in an orchestra or band of mixed winds) the alto horn has about six-and-a-half feet of tubing compared to the twelve feet of a French horn. One result of this difference in length is that the alto player does not play notes that are close together in the upper range of the instrument's harmonic series of tones. Consequently, the playing is typically more secure and can be trusted to a less experienced musician. Another result is that the alto does not have the extended range into the tenor and bass parts which can be the domain of the French horn. Brass band music from the second half of the nineteenth-century is scored for Eb horns and this sometimes leads to confusion because much of the orchestral literature of the time was also scored for Eb horns. The orchestral literature was intended for natural ("valveless") French horns or early valved "waldhorns" based on the natural horn. It was not until the end of the century that these "French" horns began to supplant the alto horn in American bands.This occurred as the brass bands evolved into ensembles of mixed winds.

**Tenors**

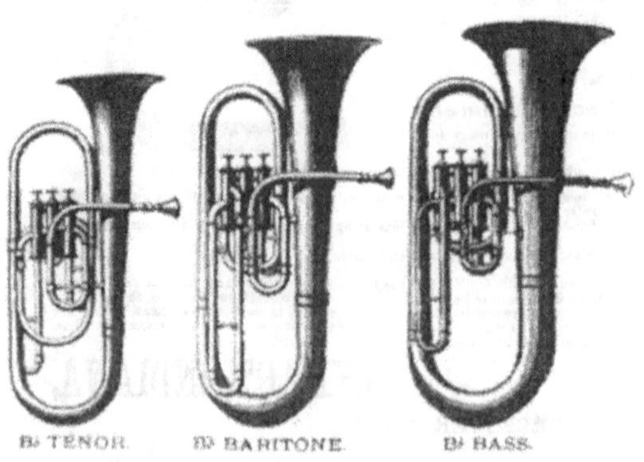

The tenor and baritone voices were played on Bb tenor horns, Bb baritone horns and trombones. These instruments incorporate about nine feet of tubing. The valved horns (members of the Saxhorn family) were more often used than the trombones, but it is not unusual to see trombones in pictures of these ensembles. The trombones had a much "brighter" sound than the more commonly-used tenor and baritone horns. The tenor horn had the least amount of conical tubing of the three valved horns. There really is no modern equivalent to this horn. The baritones were similar to our present day baritone horns. When the tubing diameter and taper was at its greatest extent on the valved horns, they were usually called basses rather than baritones. The appearance and sound of these baritone-bass horns were very similar to our present day euphoniums.

E♭ BASS

Bass parts were covered by the above-mentioned baritone-bass horns in Bb and by the larger Eb basses. The Eb bass, like the alto and baritone horns were usually upright instruments, with the over-the-shoulder models usually reserved for marching bands. This instrument was about thirteen-and-a-half feet long compared to the more common Bb tuba in a modern wind band which is nearly eighteen feet long. The larger instrument is commonly referred to as a BBb or double Bb tuba. Although the Eb instrument is not used much in the United States any longer, it is still a commonly used bass instrument in Europe. In a smaller ensemble the Eb bass is much easier to balance with the other parts, compared to the larger BBb tuba.

### The Sound

Popular valved brass instruments in the United States during the second half of the nineteenth-century sounded quite different both as solo instruments and in ensemble. The volume level was not as loud with the conical tubing and mouthpieces available at that time. The sound was more "mellow" lacking the emphasis in the upper partials or overtones. Again, this was mainly a function of the bore taper and mouthpiece design. Because the instruments and the band music were so popular, there are many good surviving collections of the instruments. We are also fortunate in the existence of a number of bands around the country who play these instruments or modern reproductions in authentic "period" ensembles. To use the original instruments is a pleasant experience but not necessarily one for which we must strive. In solo or ensemble it is certainly possible to use not only modern brass instruments, but instruments of any kind. There is no doubt that if our modern instruments were available, the arrangers would have been just as glad to play the tunes on them. This was a popular effort by musicians whose interest was in providing a joyful noise unto the Lord.

## SOURCES

### Popular Publications

In Chatfield, Minnesota, at the lending library of the Chatfield Band, one entire filing cabinet is devoted to sacred music for band. Much of it is modern, but there are many published works from the closing two decades of the nineteenth century as well. While bandleaders such as Rohr, Dignam and Leinbach were arranging and transcribing sacred music for their own hometown bands, the publisher's were having similar material produced for mass distribution by Laurendeau, Rollinson,Herbert Clarke, Levy, Barnhouse, Prendiville, Winner and most of the other names familiar to those who have taken an interest in nineteenth-century band music. The collection includes solos, duets (with keyboard as well as band accompaniment), along with small ensemble music as well

**The cover page from a nineteenth-century Barnhouse arrangement**

as the music scored for full band. The publishers include all of the major companies of the era: Schirmer, Ditson, Pepper, Church, Barnhouse, etc.

The folks at Chatfield are friendly and helpful. They are committed to doing a good job with the collection started by Jim Perkins. Write to them at PO Box 578, Chatfield, MN 55923. Best not to call because they don't have a large staff. If you have any interest in preserving a large national treasure of band music, send a big donation. The collection includes hundreds of thousands of band arrangements, including many rare pieces. This is also an important source if you find yourself missing one of the parts from a nineteenth- or early twentieth-century band arrangement.

### At Home

Have you looked in the attic of the church where you've been playing? Have you looked inside the old organ bench in the storeroom? Much of this forgotten music is around and we should bring it out. Some of it may deserve neglect but some of it is good enough to restore and strengthen your faith. We'll discover some masterpieces, too.

What follows is a small collection organized principally around the number of players that are needed, beginning with parts intended for a cornet to be used in leading the singing at a revival meeting and ending with a solo cornet accompanied by a concert band (including two clarinets). In between, the bulk of the collection is for smaller brass ensembles.

# Cornet Leader

*I can get more damn sinners weeping on a E-flat cornet than nine gospel-artists all shooting off their faces at once!* (Cornet player in Sinclair Lewis' *Elmer Gantry*)

The music in this section has been taken from the 1887 publication by The John Church Company entitled: *The Melodies of the Gospel Hymns Consolidated, arranged for the Cornet,* by S.C. Hayslip. The collection includes more than four hundred tunes taken from the popular Sankey *Gospel Hymns Consolidated, Embracing Numbers 1,2,3 and 4.* The cornet is not intended as a solo instrument in this collection but as a song leader, especially in the outdoor "meetings."

In order to select a group of hymns favored at late nineteenth-century "meetings" I have relied on the memory of Charles Ives as reported in his memoirs. No doubt he recalled his father, George, leading these tunes on his specially modified cornet!

In addition to using brass instruments to lead the singing in outdoor meetings, the music catalogs of the period indicate that the portable reed organ was also suitable for the same purpose. The portrait of Ira Sankey in the introductory chapter for our collection shows the famous song leader seated at one of these instruments. I have taken the liberty to provide keyboard parts along with the cornet parts. These parts are taken from *Gospel Hymns Consolidated* and other contemporaneous hymn books.

These particular hymns were so well known that a nineteenth century group would probably not have had to look at their hymnals for the words. Since the words were such an inseparable part of the music, I have included them here. In each instance the words are taken from the books which provided the keyboard parts.

It would be wonderful to have a large group of people to sing these hymns, led by the cornet. In addition to having the songs sung with the cornet as the song leader, it would lend an air of authenticity if the cornet was an older model with an original mouthpiece and in the "high tuning" of the day (i.e., A≠450Hz).

**A transposition problem.**

***Beulah Land*** **from the 1887 Hayslip edition.**

***Beulah Land*** **from the J.W. Pepper** ***Gospel Hymns*** **of 1887.**

Although the advertisement reproduced on page 19 claims that the arrangements for cornet from the Pepper company will match the key signatures in the Gospel Hymns, this may not have been the case. The concert key was G. The Hayslip edition correctly places a cornet in A in the key of Bb. The Pepper edition has cornet in Bb pitched in Bb.

**Beulah Land**

Rev. Edgar Page Stites

*Sorrow and sighing shall flee away* – Isaiah 35:10

1. I've reached the land of corn and wine,
And all its riches freely mine;
Here shines undimm'd one blissful day,
For all my night has pass'd away.

2. The Saviour comes and walks with me,
And sweet communion here have we;
He gently leads me with His hand,
For this is heaven's border land.

3. A sweet perfume upon the breeze,
Is borne from ever vernal trees,
And flow'rs that never fading grow,
Where streams of life forever flow.

4. The zephyrs seem to float to me,
Sweet sounds of heaven's melody,
As angels with the white-robed throng,
Join in the sweet redemption song.

Chorus:

O Beulah land, sweet Beulah land,
as on the highest mount I stand,
I look away across the sea,
where mansions are prepared for me,
And view the shining glory shore,
my heav'n, my home forever more.

## Beulah Land

from: *Gospel Hymns, No. 3* by Sankey, McGranahan, and Stebbins, 1875
and: *Gospel Hymns Consolidated, arranged for the Cornet* by S.C. Hayslip, 1887

*Sorrow and sighing shall flee away.*

Isaiah 35:10 (Headnote to the Sankey edition of this hymn in 1873)

**Just as I Am (Woodworth)**

Miss Charlottee Elliott, 1834

*Him that cometh to Me, I will in no wise cast out.* John 6: 37

1. Just as I am, without one plea,
But that Thy blood was shed for me,
And that Thou bidd'st me come to Thee,
O Lamb of God! I come, I come!

2. Just as I am, and waiting not
To rid my soul of one dark blot,
To Thee, whose blood can cleanse each spot,
O Lamb of God! I come, I come!

3. Just as I am, though tossed about,
With many a conflict, many a doubt,
Fightings and fears within, without,
O lamb of God! I come, I come!

4. Just as I am, poor, wretched, blind,
Sight, riches, healing of the mind,
Yea, all I need in Thee to find,
O Lamb of God! I come, I come!

5. Just as I am; Thou wilt receive,
Wilt welcome, pardon, cleanse, relieve;
Because Thy promise I believe,
O Lamb of God! I come, I come!

**William B. Bradbury**

# Just as I Am

from: *Gospel Hymns Consolidated (embracing volumes 1,2,3 & 4)* by Ira Sankey, *et al*. 1883.
and: *Gospel Hymns Consolidated, arranged for the Cornet* by S.C. Hayslip, 1887.

**Nearer, My God, to Thee (Bethany)**

Mrs. Sarah F. Adams, 1840

1. Nearer, my God, to Thee, Nearer to Thee!
E'en though it be a cross that raiseth me;
Still all my song shall be - Nearer, my God, to Thee-
Nearer, my God, to Thee! Nearer to Thee!

2. Though like a wanderer, the sun gone down,
Darkness be over me, my rest a stone;
Yet in my dreams I'd be – Nearer, my God, to Thee!
Nearer, my God, to Thee! Nearer to Thee!

3. There let the way appear,steps unto heaven;
All that Thou sendest me, in mercy given;
Angels to beckon me, Nearer my God to Thee-
Nearer, my God, to Thee! Nearer to Thee!

4. Then with my waking tho'ts, bright with thy praise
All that Thou sendest me, in mercy given;
So by my woes to be, Nearer my God to thee!
Nearer, my God, to Thee! Nearer to Thee!

5. Or if on joyful wing, cleaving the sky,
Sun, moon, and stars forgot, upward I fly;
Still all my song shall be - Nearer, my God, to Thee!
Nearer, my God, to Thee! Nearer to Thee!

## Nearer, My God, to Thee (Bethany)

from: *Songs of Devotion* by W. H. Doane, 1870.
and: *Gospel Hymns Consolidated, arranged for the Cornet* by S.C. Hayslip, 1887.

**The Shining Shore**

Rev. David Nelson, M.D., 1835

1. My days are gliding swiftly by,
And I, a pilgrim stranger,
Would not detain them as they fly!
Those hours of toil and danger.

CHORUS
For oh! We stand on Jordan's strand
Our friends are passing over,
And just before, the shining shore
By faith we now discover.

2. We'll gird our loins, my brethren dear,
Our distant home discerning;
Our absent Lord has left us word,
Let every lamp be burning.

3. Should coming days be cold and dark,
We need not cease our singing;
That perfect rest naught can molest,
Where golden harps are ringing.

4. Let sorrow's rudest tempests blow,
Each cord on earth to sever,
Our King says come, and there's our home,
For ever, oh! forever!

# The Shining Shore

from: *Book of Worship and Hymns and Tunes,* Lutheran Publication Society, 1899. and: *Gospel Hymns Consolidated, arranged for the Cornet* by S.C. Hayslip, 1887.

**Nettleton (Come, Thou Fount of Ev'ry Blessing)**

Rev. Robert Robinson, 1758

1. Come, Thou Fount of ev'ry blessing,
tune my heart to sing Thy grace;
Streams of mercy, never ceasing,
call for songs of loudest praise;
Teach me some melodious sonnet,
sung by flaming tongues above;
Praise the mount, – I'm fixed upon it!
Mount of Thy redeeming love.

2. Here I'll raise my Ebenezer,
hither by Thy help I'm come;
And I hope by Thy good pleasure,
safely to arrive at home.
Jesus sought me when a stranger,
wandering from the fold of God!
He, to rescue me from danger,
interposed his precious blood.

3. Oh, to grace how great a debtor,
daily I'm constrained to be!
Let Thy goodness as a fetter,
bind my wandering heart to thee.

## Nettleton

from: *Repository of Sacred Music, Part Second* by John Wyeth, 1813.
and: *Gospel Hymns Consolidated, arranged for the Cornet* by S.C. Hayslip, 1887.

## Sweet By-and-By

*The ransomed of the Lord shall return and come to Zion with songs and everlasting joy upon their heads.* Isaiah 35: 10.
(headnote to the Sankey edition of 1875)

Sanford Fillmore Bennett, M.D., 1867

1. There's a land that is fairer than day,
and by faith we can see it a-far;
For the Father waits over the way,
to prepare us a dwelling place there.

2. We shall sing on that beautiful shore,
the melodious songs of the blest,
And our spirit shall sorrow no more,
not a sigh for the blessing of rest.

3. To our bountiful Father above,
we will offer our tribute of praise,
For the glorious gift of His love,
and the blessings that hallow our days.

CHORUS

In the sweet by-and-by,
we shall meet on that beautiful shore,
In the sweet by-and-by,
we shall meet on that beautiful shore.

## Sweet By-and-By

from: *Winnowed Hymns* by Hubert P. Main, 1873.
and: *Gospel Hymns Consolidated, arranged for the Cornet* by S.C. Hayslip, 1887.

Joseph P. Webster, 1867

## AUTHORS AND COMPOSERS

The author of the text is listed first, composer of the tune is listed second.

### *Beulah Land*

Rev. Edgar Page Stites (1836-1921). Stites was a Civil War veteran, riverboat pilot and missionary to the frontier churches in South Dakota.

Jno (John H.) R. Sweney (1837-1899). Composer of many hymns and professor of music at the Pennsylvania Military Academy. He played cornet and led the band of the Third Delaware Regiment during the Civil War. This song was sung at his funeral by Ira Sankey.

### *Just as I Am (Woodworth)*

Charlotte Elliot (1789-1871). As an invalid, Charlotte Elliot wrote this hymn in 1834 in the midst of a depression as an attempt to express reasons to trust in Christ. She wrote the hymn for sale as a contribution to the establishment of a school for poor children. Early printings always included the text from John below the hymn title.

William B. Bradbury (1816-1868). Bradbury was a music teacher, editor of the *New York Musical Review*, organist, composer, publisher, and author of *The Jubilee* (1858) which sold more than 200,000 copies. He was a student of Lowell Mason and one of the important early publishers of Sunday School music.

### *Nearer, My God, to Thee (Bethany)*

Sarah F. Adams (1805-1848). Sarah Adams was a talented journalist who lived in London. This hymn first appeared in a Unitarian collection entitled *Hymns and Anthems* published locally by her church in 1840-41.

Lowell Mason (1792-1872). Raised in a family of amateur musicians, Mason was also a nineteenth century entrepreneur much admired by his contemporaries. Some of his famous and successful collections of sacred music included: *The Boston Handel and Haydn Society Collection of Church Music; Carmina Sacra; Juvenile Psalmist; The Hallelujah.* "Of all musicians active in the United States during the nineteenth century, Lowell Mason has left the strongest, the widest, and the most lasting impress on our musical culture." [32]

*The Shining Shore*

Rev. David Nelson, M.D. (1793-1844). Nelson gave up the practice of medicine to become a Presbyterian minister. He was a member of the Missionary Society and active in the anti-slavery movement.

George F. Root (1820-1895). Like his teacher, Lowell Mason, George Root was an important figure in nineteenth century American music. His enormous output included both sacred and secular music such as this hymn tune and the civil war song: *The Battle Cry of Freedom*. The greater part of his career was spent in Chicago where he was associated with his brother's company, Root & Cady.

*Nettleton (Come, Thou Fount of Ev'ry Blessing)*

Rev. Robert Robinson (1735-1790). He was converted in a revival by George Whitefield. Ordained as an English Methodist clergyman, he later became a Baptist, an Independent and finally a Socinian.

John Wyeth (1792-1858). Wyeth was a musician and publisher of *Wyeth's Repository of Sacred Music* (1810) and *Repository of Sacred Music, Part Second* (1813). *Part Second* is important as a source of American folk hymnody "intended . . . for use at revivals and camp meetings . . . Most of the southern tune-book compilers . . . borrowed extensively from . . . Wyeth's collection." [33] The sound of *Nettleton* clearly sets it apart from the work of his contemporary New Englanders. It is startling to realize that Wyeth was born near Boston and worked in Philadelphia. It is also fascinating that the imaginative memory of Charles Ives would bring this tune up alongside the other five tunes in his recollection.

*Sweet By-and-By*

Sanford Fillmore Bennett, M.D. (1836-1898). Born in upstate New York, Bennett was a pharmacist and physician in Wisconsin. He served as a Lieutenant during the Civil War. He collaborated on a Sunday School hymnbook entitled *The Signet Ring* (1868) with his friend Joseph Webster.

Joseph P. Webster (1819-1875). As an active member of the Boston *Handel and Haydn Society* early in the century, Webster must have been acquainted with and influenced by Lowell Mason. He moved to Wisconsin in 1856. After writing this hymn with Bennett and having it published privately, he tried to sell it - first to Root & Cady in Chicago, who turned it down, and then successfully to Lyon and Healy (for $20.00). It became enormously popular once Ira Sankey began to use it on the Revival circuit and reprinted it in his hymn books in the early 1870s.

# Small Ensembles

The word *ensemble* is used to avoid confusion. In the nineteenth century the groups would most likely have been called bands. The idea of a band was even less standardized in those days than it is now. For a long time, at least until after the Civil War, the term was most often applied to a small group of brasswinds. It was not until late in the nineteenth century that the woodwinds began to approach their modern numbers in amateur bands. The size of a band tended to be much smaller than the bands of today. An "ideal" complement according to instrument manufacturer's catalogs was a "band of twelve" comprised of seven brasswinds, two woodwinds and three percussionists.[34] When the publishers began to respond to the demand for music which had heretofore usually been provided in manuscript by the local bandleader/arranger, they usually advertised arrangements as being available in editions from quartet up to and including "full band" (see the advertisement for Pepper's *Gospel Hymns Sacred Band Book* reproduced in the Introduction ).

The music in this section was found in both published and manuscript collections. *Adagio Religioso* was published in 1892 as part of a brass quartet album arranged by Harry Prendiville (1848-1910) under the pseudonym Paul de Ville. Prendiville came to the U.S. from England in the late 1870s and settled in Ware, Massachusetts. He wrote and arranged more than 2,500 works. "The best of the celebrated Jules Levy solos came from the pen of Prendiville."[35] Our selection was scored for a combination of three cornets and baritone horn or four cornets. *Rejoice and be glad* was scored for a more common quartet of two cornets, alto and baritone horns by Louis-Phillippe Laurendeau in 1902. Laurendeau (1861-1916) was a Canadian born arranger of a prodigious amount of music. He was an editor for Carl Fischer for over thirty years. The tune is attributed to John Jenkins Husband (1760-1825), a musician and church clerk in Philadelphia during the early nineteenth century.

The important Moravian collection transmitted to us by Bernard Pfohl's edition is represented here by six hymns closely associated with their band traditions in the Southern Province of the Moravian Church. A seventh Moravian arrangement has been taken from a collection edited in 1905 by Adelaide Fries and found in the New York City Public Library.[36]

A much earlier piece, *Wo mit soll ich dich,* is from manuscript parts copies in the music archives of Old Economy Village, Pennsylvania. The set of parts seems reasonably complete and includes: two cornets, alto, trombone, baritone and tuba. The parts are unsigned, but may be the work of either Benjamin or Henry Feucht who were cornet players and members of the community band in the 1850s and 1860s. The Feuchts left the communal society in 1865,[37] so if the arrangement is theirs, then it probably predates the work of the Moravian Edward Leinbach, represented by the six arrangements of Bernard Pfohl.

**Brass choir playing from the church tower. Photo courtesy of the Lititz Moravian Congregation, Lititz, PA.**

# FUNERAL CHORALS
OF THE
# UNITAS FRATRUM
OR
# MORAVIAN CHURCH

## THE TROMBONE CHOIR.

Among the beautiful customs which the modern Moravian Church has inherited from the fervent days in Herrnhut in the Zinzendorf era, there is none more distinctive or more beautiful than the use of trombones and other wind instruments to announce the death of a member of the Moravian Church, and to accompany the burial services.

Probably the custom was a gradual growth, keeping pace with the development of the Moravian congregations, and their division into "Choirs," a term which was not only used to signify a company of singers, but also certain other groups of persons who were closely banded together by mutual interests for a common purpose. Thus the association of trombonists was known as the Trombone Choir, while the Congregation itself was divided into choirs of married people, widows, and widowers, the choir of "single brethren" or unmarried men over eighteen years of age, the choir of "older boys" between fourteen and eighteen years old, the similar choirs of "single sisters" and "older girls," and the choir of children.

Just when trombones were introduced into Herrnhut does not appear. The first Easter service on the graveyard, at four o'clock in the morning of April 13, 1732, consisted of songs, and there is no record of instrumental music, but the Moravian emigrants to Georgia in 1735 took trombones and French horns. The diary of the Moravian Congregation in Savannah does not say how the trombones were used, but does state that when the Indian Chief Tomochichi died, the Moravians refused a request from General Oglethorpe to furnish trombone music at his funeral,—an idea which would scarcely have occurred to the General had the Moravians not so accompanied the interment of their own dead.

The origin of the announcement of a member's death by the trombones is also obscure. It was practiced in many of the German State churches where it corresponded to the tolling of bells elsewhere, and since there were so many distinct "Choirs" in the Moravian Congregation, it was natural that a special tune should come to be assigned to each. Rev. C. A. Haehnle, of Nazareth, Pa., suggests that the schedule of tunes may have been arranged by Christian Gregor, a hymn-writer and skilled musician, who joined the Unitas Fratrum in 1742, served various congregations as organist until 1764, and filled important offices until his death in 1801. At least it seems safe to say that the use of trombones at funerals was established prior to 1736, and that the sys-

This illustration is taken from the cover and page 3 of Adelaide L. Fries' book: *Funeral Chorales of the Unitas Fratrum or Moravian Church.*

tem of announcement hymns was elaborated before Zinzendorf's death in 1760. The full set of tunes and stanzas was printed in the German Moravian Liturgy Book of 1791, and subsequent editions, but they may well have been used long before that time.

The use of trombones is not universal throughout the modern Moravian Church. There are no Trombone Choirs in the English and many of the American congregations, nor on the mission fields, but wherever there is such a choir the music is highly prized, not only in connection with funerals but for the Easter services and other special occasions. The Moravian churches in Germany, and certain in America, cherish their Trombone Choirs, and with one exception all are still using the tunes selected in Herrnhut in the eighteenth century to announce the death of a member of the Congregation. In the stanzas associated with those tunes there have been some changes from time to time, but practically none in the thoughts expressed. The German stanzas have been published in Liturgy Books of various dates, while translations by Rev. C. A. Haehnle were printed in *The Moravian* about 1882. Other translations by Mr. F. W. Detterer, revised by Rt. Rev. J. Mortimer Levering, appear in *The Hand-book of the Moravian Congregation of Bethlehem*, 1891; and the stanzas used at Lititz are given on a card issued in 1902. On the following pages appear the stanzas now accepted in Herrnhut, Bethlehem, and Salem, as representing the German and the American Moravian Churches.

The announcement of a death has three distinct features. The Trombone Choir, stationed in the belfry or before the Church, plays a tune, the associated stanza referring to the departure of a member of the Congregation. This is followed by a tune which indicates to which "Choir" of the Congregation the deceased belonged, the married brethren, married sisters, widowers, widows, single brethren, single sisters, older boys, older girls, little boys, and little girls each having a special tune and stanza. After this the first tune is repeated, but with reference to another stanza, one which reminds the hearer that the Death Angel will some day come to him.

From the first there was much latitude allowed as to the hymns used during the burial services, various chorals being rendered when the congregation assembled in front of the church after the funeral discourse, as the procession passed to the graveyard, and during the interment. The chorals which follow are used in Salem, North Carolina, at the present time, and they are given to complete the series, and to show the faith and hope in which departing members are laid to rest in the quiet squares of the Moravian "God's Acre."

ADELAIDE L. FRIES.

Winston-Salem, N. C., 1905.

This illustration is taken from the cover and pages 4 and 5 of Adelaide L. Fries' book: *Funeral Chorales of the Unitas Fratrum or Moravian Church.*

# Morning Star, O Cheering Sight

## Chorales and Tunes Used by the Bands of The Moravian Church

# Old Hundredth

**Chorales and Tunes Used by the Bands of the Moravian Church**

## Martha (Jesus, Lover of My Soul)

### Chorales and Tunes Used by the Bands of the Moravian Church

John Beck Hammer, 1871
Arr. Bernard Pfohl

## Sing Hallelujah (Praise the Lord!)

### Chorales and Tunes Used by the Bands of the Moravian Church

John Christian Bechler, c. 1830
Arr. Bernard Pfohl

## Fierce Was the Wild Billow

### Chorales and Tunes Used by the Bands of the Moravian Church

Gioacchino Antonio Rossini
Arr. Bernard Pfohl

ff
ff
ff
ff
ff
1.
2.
p
pp
rall.
p
pp
p
pp
p
pp
p
pp
p
pp
p
pp
p
pp
p
pp
p
pp

## How Shall I Meet (My Saviour?)
### Chorales and Tunes Used by the Bands of the Moravian Church

Edward W. Leinbach, 1870
Arr. Bernard Pfohl

# Passion Chorale

*Funeral Chorales of the Unitas Fratrum*

edited by Adelaide Fries

Hans Leo Hassler, 1601

**The original manuscripts for *Wo mit soll ich dich*. Courtesy of the Old Economy Village Archives, Pennsylvania Historical and Museum Commission.**

## Wo mit soll ich dich

**from manuscripts (c. 1850) in the Music Archives of Old Economy Village, PA**

## Rejoice and be glad

C. Fischer's Collection of Gospel Hymns
arranged by L. P. Laurendeau, 1902

J.J. Husband, 1874

## Adagio Religioso

*Excelsior Brass Quartette Album*

arranged by Paul de Ville, 1892

Solo.
ff
pp
mf
p

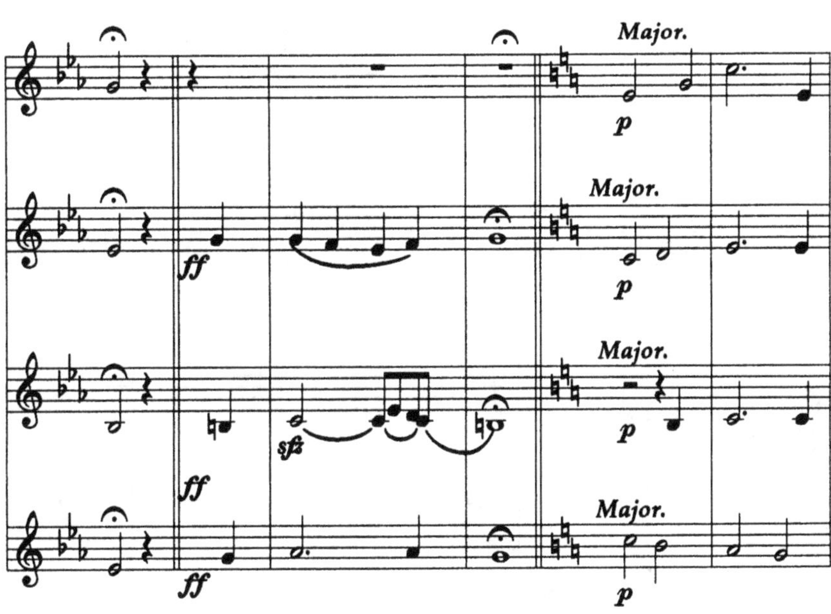
Major.
p
Major.
ff
p
Major.
sfz
ff
p
Major.
ff
p

mf

p

p
pp
Fine
pp
Fine

# Large Ensembles

The sextet, *Wo mit soll ich dich,* might serve as a transition between the smaller ensemble pieces and what we would more nearly identify as a brass band in the twentieth century. The first two works for larger brass ensembles are octets, and both of these are also from the manuscript collection in Old Economy Village. Unlike the small, loose pieces of paper on which *Wo mit soll ich dich* was jotted, *Lobe den herren* and *Wir der hiesz* are carefully written and bound into a large bandmaster's book with the inscription: "Mr. Henry Feicht's book/Bolivar Ohio." It is tempting to speculate that this Henry Feicht may have been the Henry "Feucht" who had moved to Ohio after leaving the commune and that he then brought his book back with him

**Manuscript score of *Lobe den herren.* Courtesy of the Old Economy Village Music Archives, Pennsylvania Historical and Museum Commission**

during an attempted reconciliation in the 1880s.

After the Civil War and sometime after the Feichts left the commune at Economy, Pennsylvania, the community hired a German immigrant named Jacob Rohr to be their bandmaster and music teacher. Although Rohr led the Economy Band from the late 1870s to the early 1890s, he never joined the commune. He was a prolific composer and arranger. In the archives at Old Economy Village there is an extended suite for band entitled: *Reccolections* (sic) *of War and Peace* which I think is probably the work of Jacob Rohr. One of the themes in the piece is a treatment of Webster's well-known *Sweet By-and-By.* The popular response line in the bass is here provided with much more melodic fluidity by Rohr in the tuba part.

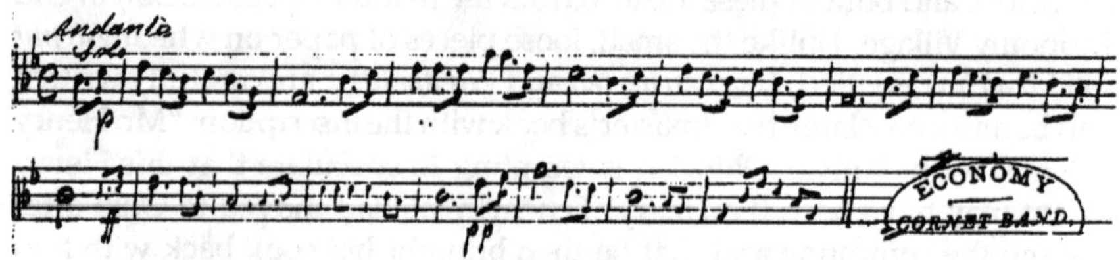


**Selection from the solo cornet manuscript with the *Sweet By-and-By* theme. Courtesy of the Old Economy Village Music Archives, Pennsylvania Historical and Museum Commission**

Prior to the Civil War, in Manchester, New Hampshire, Walter Dignam was working both as a church organist and a bandmaster. His manuscript collection includes complete band books for a brass band. Among his sacred tunes in the collection is a little known alternative tune to the familiar Christmas carol *Joy to the World* called *St. Martins.* St. Martins was written by an Englishman named William Tans'ur in the mid-eighteenth century. Paul Maybery, the musicologist, bandmaster and authority on nineteenth century band practices, dates this collection from the 1850s.

## Lobe den herren

*Mr. Henry Feicht's book*

Bolivar, Ohio c. 1860

*Wir der hiesz.* Manuscript courtesy of the Old Economy Village Music Archives, Pennsylvania Historical and Museum Commission.

## Wir der hiesz

*Mr. Henry Feicht's Book*

Bolivar, Ohio c. 1860

3
3

Divi

## Sweet By-and-By

*Recollections of War and Peace*

Jacob Rohr, c. 1875

8va
(f)
f
ff
ff
f
f
f
f
f

8va
(pp)
pp
(pp)
pp
(pp)
(pp)
p
pp
(pp)

## St. Martins

*Walter Digman's Band Books*
c. 1853

# Solos

The cornet parts in section II (Cornet Leader) are not solos but leaders parts. However there is an extensive literature of solos and duets for brass, usually accompanied by piano or band. Often the music would be available with either kind of accompaniment. Frequently there would be editions of the same piece for either cornet, baritone (euphonium), or trombone. As with all of this music, publishing companies in the latter part of the century distributed music which was earlier provided on location in manuscript.

*Vesper Hymn* is a lovely setting for cornet and piano of a tune arranged by T.H. Rollinson (1844-1928). Like Dignam, Rollinson was both a church organist and bandmaster who spent most of his professional life in the same place, in this instance, Waltham, Massachusetts. Unlike Dignam, most of Rollinson's tremendous output was published by the major music publishers including Cundy, Ditson, Pepper and Fischer. This particular piece was published by Cundy in 1884.

A completely different kind of solo literature is represented here by an arrangement of *Pleyel's Hymn* from the Economy archives. This arrangement may be the work of Jacob Rohr or of his successor John S. Duss. As with the arrangement of *Sweet By-and-By, Pleyel's Hymn* is for a large ensemble and includes parts for two clarinets as well as for ten brasswinds and percussion. The peaceful beauty of the theme developed in a solo like *Vesper Hymn* is forgone here in order to demonstrate the virtuosity of the soloist. For those brass players trained using the Arban *Method,* the *air varié* is a familiar routine, and I suspect that even devout believers, on hearing this arrangement, may have questioned its sanctity. Nonetheless, it is not an exceptional representative of its kind. Commercial publications of the period include the popular *Rock of Ages* presented in the same format. The C.L. Barnhouse solo cornet part for that hymn arrangement is reproduced here. Barnhouse (1865-1929) was a remarkable man. In 1884 he was a professional cornet soloist. His publishing business, established c. 1895 in Oskaloosa, Iowa is still a large business operated by his grandchildren.

Solo part from the 1903 Barnhouse publication of *Rock of Ages.*

# Vesper Hymn

*Cundy's Evening Companion*

arranged by T.H. Rollinson, 1884

f
f

# Pleyel's Hymn

*Variations for Cornet*

from manuscript probably by Jacob Rohr, c. 1875

Cadenza
a poco rall. . . .
tr
Cad.
Cad.
Cad.
Cad.
Cad.
Cad.
Cad.
Cad.
Cad.
Cad.
Cad.
Cad.
Cad.

Moderato
p
pp
pp
pp
mf
pp
p

Tutti I
Tutti I
Tutti I
Tutti I
Tutti I
ff
Tutti I
ff
Tutti I
ff
Tutti I
ff
Tutti I
ff
Tutti I
ff
Tutti I
Tutti I
ff
Tutti I
Tutti I
f

ff
ff

Var. I
Var. I
Var. I
Var. I
pp
Var. I
Var. I
pp
Var. I
pp
Var. I
pp
Var. I
pp
Var. I
pp
Var. I
Var. I
pp
Var. I
Var. I

pp
p
p
p
p
p

1.
2.
pp
pp
pp
pp

Tutti II Dance
Tempo di Schottische
Tempo di Schottische
f Tutti II Schottische
ff Tutti II Tempo di Schottische
Tutti II Schottische
Tutti II Tempo di Schottische
f Tutti II Schottische
Tutti II Schottische
f Tutti II Tempo di Schottische
Tutti II Tempo di Schottische
Tutti II Tempo di Schottische
Tutti II Schottische
Tutti II

3
3
3
3
3
3

Var. II
Var. II
Var. II
Var. II
pp
Var. II
pp
Var. II
pp
Var. II
Var. II
mf
Var. II
p
Var. II
Var. II

p
p
p
p
p
p

Tutti III
Tutti III
ff
Tutti III
f
Tutti III Tempo March
f
Tutti III
ff
Tutti III
ff
Tutti III
pp
f
Tutti III
p
f
Tutti III
pp
f
Tutti III
f
Tutti III
f
Tutti III
ff
Tutti III
f
Tutti III
f

ff

1.
2.
Cadenza
Cadenza
Cadenza
Cornet cadenza ⊕(alto follows)
Cornet cadenza ⊕(alto follows)

Var. III
Var. III
Var. III
Var. III
Var. III
Var. III
Var. III
Var. III
p
Var. III
Var. III
Var. III
pp
Var. III
Var. III
Var. III

6
6
6
6
6
6
6

pp

Finale
6
6
6
6
6
6
3
3
Finale
ff
Finale
ff
Finale
f
Finale
Finale
ff
Finale
Finale
f
Finale
f
Finale
f
Finale
ff
Finale
f
Finale
Finale

6
6
3
3
6
6

3
6
3
6
3
6
p

3
6
f
f

# Postlude and Notes

Many of us have been steeped in the old idea that instrumental music, especially music for brass, was not something generally accepted in churches in the United States during bygone days. The plain fact of the matter is that then as now there were widely differing points of view and practices. We know that the Moravians brought with them their time honored traditions surrounding the sacramental use of brass. Even a cursory look at publisher's advertisements in the nineteenth century reveals that much material was being produced that was suitable for church bands and orchestras. Both liturgical and non-liturgical churches had room for this music as is evidenced by the extant works. In addition to playing in the church, brasswinds were especially in demand for outdoor events, including revival meetings and Sunday School picnics.

As the turn of the century drew near, the secularization of American culture began in earnest. We begin to see the "sacred" music being used for the quiet, serious and contemplative interludes in the purely secular concerts of the professional bands. Emulation of the professionals and their practices by the amateur town bands contributed to the rapid increase in the size of the bands, the numbers of woodwinds in the bands, and a dissociation from the great wellspring of traditional sacred music for brasswinds in the United States.

1 Gilbert Chase, *America's Music* (New York, 1955), pp. 44-45.
2 Lucius L. Shattuck to his brother 3 May 1863, as cited by Bufkin, "Union Bands of the Civil War . . ." Ph.D. dissertation, LSU, 1973. Quoted by Kenneth E. Olson in *Music and Musket* (Westport, Conn., 1981), p. 192.
3 Bernard J. Pfohl, *The Salem Band* (Winston-Salem, N.C., 1953).
4 Chase, op cit., p. 162.
5 Pfohl, op cit., pp. 14, 51-52.
6 Theron Brown and Hezekiah Butterworth, *The Story of the Hymns and Tunes* (New York, 1906), pp. 155, 157, 424-425, etc.
7 Ibid., p. 425.
8 Pfohl, op cit., pp. 51-52.

9 Robert R. Roberts, "Gilt, Gingerbread, and Realism: The Public and Its Taste," in H. Wayne Morgan, ed., *The Gilded Age, A Reappraisal*. (Syracuse, 1963), pp. 169-195.
10 William Arms Fisher, *One Hundred and Fifty Years of Music Publishing in the United States* (Boston, 1933), p. 59.
11 Albert Edward Bailey, *The Gospel in Hymns*, (New York, 1950), p. 483.
12 Ibid., p. 484, citing L.F. Benson.
13 S.C. Hayslip, *The Melodies of Gospel Hymns Consolidated, arranged for the Cornet* (Cincinnati, 1887).
14 Charles E. Ives, *Memos* (New York, 1972), pp. 131-133, John Kirkpatrick, ed.
15 J.W. Pepper, *J.W. Pepper's Complete Catalogue* (Philadelphia, 1907), p. 66.
16 LeRoi Jones, *Blues People* (New York, 1963), p. 47.
17 Chase, op cit., p. 237.
18 William Schafer, *Brass Bands and New Orleans Jazz* (Louisiana, 1977).
19 Ibid., p. 477.
20 Ibid., p. 74.
21 Richard D. Wetzel, *Frontier Musicians on the Connoquenessing, Wabash, and Ohio* (Ohio, 1976), p. 140.
22 Ibid., p. 99.
23 The well-known scholar and conductor, Paul Maybery of St. Paul, has called the Dignam collection ". . . perhaps the finest and most substantial of all known American brass band collections." (Liner notes to: The Yankee Brass Band, New World Records, 1981.)
24 Irving Sablosky, *What They Heard: Music in America, 1852-1881 from the Pages of Dwight's Journal of Music* (Louisiana, 1986), p. 65.
25 In his Journal . . . of July 3, 1869, Dwight says, among other things: That the . . . brain of the greatest musical festival in all the ages should be, not [a] . . . great musical man of any sort, . . . but a Gilmore, a clever leader of a local band . . . later, reporting on the performance at the Jubilee of Handel's Let the Bright Seraphim he writes: With [Matthew] Arbuckle's [cornet] obligato (one longs for the real crackling old-fashioned trumpet though) it made great effect, by no means so great as it would be in a smaller hall . . .
26 Kenneth Kreitner, *Discoursing Sweet Music: Town Bands and Community Life in Turn-of-the-Century Pennsylvania* (Illinois, 1990), p. 80 ff.
27 Ibid., p. 91.
28 Ibid., p. 81.
29 Ronald W. Holz, *Heralds of Victory* (New York, 1986), p. 194.
30 1914. It is interesting to note that Charles Ives began a listing of his works on the back of a 1928 calendar. The list includes much church music from the 1880s and 90s as well as: "Brass Band: . . . Slow March (Adeste

Fidelis, cantus firmus) '86 or 87, played by Danbury Band, and . . . Carmel, N.Y. Band. . . . Fantasia (or Paraphrase) on Jerusalem the Golden (before leaving Stevens St. Danbury, 1888)." In a later list he included: "Chorals from a "Harvest Festival" for double chorus, organ, trumpets, trombones. . . 1897"

31 Norman Smith in *March Music Notes* (Program Note Press, Lake Charles, LA, 1986) notes that the music William Himes is available to ensembles other than just the Salvation Army. Certainly his setting of Nicaea and his march Invictus are well worth the effort of looking them up.

32 Chase, op cit., p. 151.

33 Ibid., p. 189.

34 Kreitner, op cit., pp. 144-145.

35 William R. Baker in Rehrig and Bierley, *The Heritage Encyclopedia of Band Music* (Ohio, 1991), p. 603.

36 Adelaide L. Fries, *Funeral Chorales of the Unitas Fratrum or Moravian Church* (Winston-Salem, N.C., c. 1905), pp. 6, 17-18.

37 Wetzel, op cit., p. 95. An excellent recording of *Wo mit soll ich dich* has been made by the Chestnut Brass Company (Listen to the Mocking Bird, Newport Classic CD, NPD 85516, 1991).

# Bibliography


Bailey, Albert Edward. *The Gospel in Hymns*. New York: Scribner's, 1950.

Bird, Ruth Holmes. *Music Among the Moravians*. New York: University of Rochester microcard c. 1958), 1938.

Blume, Friedrich. *Protestant Church Music*. New York: W.W. Norton, 1974.

Bonner, D.F. *Instrumental Music in the Worship of God*. Rochester, New York: F.A. Capwell, 1881.

Boon, Brindley. *Play the Music, Play!* London, England: The Salvation Army, 1966.

Bradbury, Wm. B. *The Victory*. New York: Biglow & Main, 1869.

Brown, Theron, and Butterworth, Hezekiah. *The Story of the Hymns and Tunes*. New York: American Tract Society, 1906.

Bryant, Carolyn. *And the Band Played On*. Washington, D.C.: Smithsonian Institution, 1975.

Chase, Gilbert. *America's Music*. New York: McGraw-Hill, 1955.

Elrod, Mark, and Garofalo, Robert. *A Pictorial History of Civil War Era Musical Instruments and Military Bands*. Charleston, West Virginia: Pictorial Histories Publishing Company, 1985.

Fisher, William Arms. *One Hundred and Fifty Years of Music Publishing in the United States*. Boston: Ditson Company, 1933.

Fries, Adelaide L. *Funeral Chorales of the Unitas Fratrum or Moravian Church*. Winston-Salem, North Carolina: no publisher, c. 1905.

Hartzell, Lawrence W. *Ohio Moravian Music*. Winston-Salem, North Carolina: The Moravian Music Foundation Press (London and Toronto, Associated University Presses), 1988.

Hayslip, S.C. *The Melodies of Gospel Hymns Consolidated, arranged for the Cornet*. Cincinnati, New York: The John Church Co. and New York, Chicago: Biglow & Main, 1887.

Hazen, Margret Hindle, and Robert M. *The Music Men*. Washington, D.C.: Smithsonian Institution, 1987.

Hillman, Joseph. *The Revivalist*. Troy, New York: Joseph Hillman, 1869.

Holz, Ronald W. *Heralds of Victory*. New York: The Salvation Army, 1986.

____. *A History of the Hymn Tune Meditation and Related Forms in Salvation Army Instrumental Music in Great Britain and North America, 1880-1980*. Ann Arbor, Michigan: University Microfilms International, 1981.

Ives, Charles E. (John Kirkpatrick, ed.). *Memos*. New York: W.W. Norton & Company, 1972.

Jones, LeRoi. *Blues People*. New York: William Morrow and Company, 1963.

Keehn, David P. *The Trombone Choir of the Moravian Church in North America*. Unpublished report, (338 pp.). West Chester State College, Pennsylvania, 1978.

Kreitner, Kenneth. *Discoursing Sweet Music: Town Bands and Community Life in Turn-of-the-Century Pennsylvania*. Illinois: University of Illinois, 1990.

Lewis, Sinclair. *Elmer Gantry*. New York: Harcourt, Brace and Company, 1927.

Lutheran Publication Society. *Book of Worship*. Philadelphia: General Synod of the Evangelical Lutheran Church in the United States, 1899.

McQuaid, Wm. P. Rt. Rev., Mon. *Memoir of Reverend William McDonald*. Mt. St. Mary's: ?, 1909.

Mellers, Wilfrid. *Music in a New Found Land*. New York: Stonehill, 1964.

Moravian Church in America, The. *Hymnal and Liturgies of the Moravian Church*. Illinois: The Moravian Church in America Northern and Southern Provinces, 1969.

Ode, James A. *Brass Instruments in Church Services*. Minneapolis, Minnesota: Augsburg Publishing House, 1970.

Olson, Kenneth E. *Music and Musket*. Westport, Connecticut: Greenwood Press, 1981.

Pepper, J.W. *J.W. Pepper's Complete Catalogue*. Philadelphia: J.W. Pepper, 1907.

Pfohl, Bernard. *Chorales and Tunes Used by the Bands of The Moravian Church*. Winston-Salem, North Carolina: Bernard Pfohl, 1927.

______. *The Salem Band*. Winston-Salem, North Carolina: Bernard Pfohl, 1953.

Rehrig, William H., and Bierley, Paul (ed.). *The Heritage Encyclopedia of Band Music*. Westerville, Ohio: Integrity Press, 1991.

Robinson, Chas. S. *Songs for the Sanctuary*. New York and Chicago: A.S. Barnes & Company, 1873.

Rogal, Samuel J. *Sing Glory and Hallelujah! Historical and Biographical Guide to Gospel Hymns Nos. 1 to 6 Complete*. Westport, Connecticut: Greenwood Press, 1996.

Sablosky, Irving. *What They Heard: Music in America, 1852-1881 from the Pages of Dwight's Journal of Music*. Baton Rouge, Louisiana: Louisiana University, 1986.

Salvation Army. *Salvation Army Band Journal*. London, England: The Salvation Army, 1884.

Sankey, Ira D., Bliss, P. P., McGranahan, James, and Stebbins, George C. *Gospel Hymns Consolidated.* New York, Chicago, Cincinnati: The Biglow & Main Co. and The John Church Co., 1883.

Schafer, William. *Brass Bands and New Orleans Jazz.* Baton Rouge, Louisiana: Louisiana University, 1977.

Schwartz, H.W. *Bands of America.* New York: Doubleday, 1957.

Sims, Patsy. *Can Somebody Shout Amen!* New York: St. Martin's Press, 1988.

Smith, Norman. E. *March Music Notes.* Lake Charles, Louisiana: Program Note Press, 1986.

Steelman, Robert. *Catalog of the Lititz Congregation Collection.* Chapel Hill, North Carolina: The University of North Carolina, 1981.

Stevenson, Robert. *Protestant Church Music in America.* New York: W.W. Norton, 1966.

Wetzel, Richard D. *Frontier Musicians on the Connoquenessing, Wabash, and Ohio.* Athens, Ohio: Ohio University Press, 1976.

White, B. F., and King, E.J. *The Sacred Harp.* Philadelphia: Collins, 1844.

# Index

**About the Author**

MARK J. ANDERSON is a freelance writer and musician who lives in Woodstock, New York. He is a frequent contributor to national and international music journals. He also teaches music and leads brass ensembles for a religious community.

**Recent Titles in**
**the Music Reference Collection**

Musical Anthologies for Analytical Study: A Bibliography
*James E. Perone, compiler*

A Guide to Popular Music Reference Books: An Annotated Bibliography
*Gary Haggerty*

Rock Music Scholarship: An Interdisciplinary Bibliography
*Jeffrey N. Gatten*

Sing Glory and Hallelujah!: Historical and Biographical Guide to
*Gospel Hymns Nos. 1 to 6 Complete*
*Samuel J. Rogal, compiler*

Orchestration Theory: A Bibliography
*James E. Perone, compiler*

Brass Music of Black Composers: A Bibliography
*Aaron Horne, compiler*

The Music and Dance of the World's Religions: A Comprehensive, Annotated Bibliography of Materials in the English Language
*E. Gardner Rust*

Twentieth-Century American Music for the Dance: A Bibliography
*Isabelle Emerson, compiler and editor*

Electronic and Computer Music
*Robert L. Wick*

Harmony Theory: A Bibliography
*James E. Perone, compiler*

A Mozart Diary: A Chronological Reconstruction of the Composer's Life, 1761–1791
*Peter Dimond, compiler*

The Grateful Dead and the Deadheads: An Annotated Bibliography
*David G. Dodd and Robert G. Weiner*

www.ingramcontent.com/pod-product-compliance
Lightning Source LLC
Chambersburg PA
CBHW060349100426
42812CB00003B/1176

* 9 7 8 0 3 1 3 3 0 3 8 0 7 *